Ready for Life

Book Five:

How to Know What God Wants

VICTOR BOOKS
A DIVISION OF SCRIPTURE PRESS PUBLICATIONS INC.
USA CANADA ENGLAND

Ready for Life

Book Five:

How to Know What God Wants

Karen Dockrey
Kevin Johnson
Bob Krafft
Greg Lafferty
Tom Nummela
Mark Oestreicher
Ginny Olson
Dave Veerman, Series Editor

Titles in This Series:
- How to Be a Good Friend
- How to Get Along with the Opposite Sex
- How to Teach Your Parents
- How to Win in Life
- How to Know What God Wants
- How to Explain What You Believe

Scripture, unless otherwise indicated, is taken from the *HOLY BIBLE, NEW INTERNATIONAL VERSION®*. Copyright © 1973, 1978, 1984 by International Bible Society. Used by permission of Zondervan Publishing House. All rights reserved. The "NIV" and *"New International Version"* trademarks are registered in the United States Patent and Trademark Office by International Bible Society. Use of either trademark requires the permission of International Bible Society.

Verses marked TLB are taken from *The Living Bible*, copyright © 1971. Used by permission of Tyndale House Publishers, Inc., Wheaton, IL 60189. All rights reserved.

This book was produced with the assistance of The Livingstone Corporation, David R. Veerman, Daryl J. Lucas, Claudia Gerwin, and Brenda James Todd, project staff.

Structural Editing: David R. Veerman

Copyediting: Daryl J. Lucas, Claudia Gerwin

Cover Design: Joe DeLeon

Typesetting: Brenda James Todd

ISBN: 1-56476-091-X

©1994 by SP Publications, Inc. All rights reserved. Printed in the United States of America.

1 2 3 4 5 6 7 8 9 10 Printing/Year 98 97 96 95 94

Permission is granted to reproduce charts, diagrams, and clip art for use in promotion and group study. No other part of this book may be reproduced without written permission, except for brief quotations in books and critical reviews. For information, write Victor Books, 1825 College Avenue, Wheaton, IL 60187.

Contents

Only the Best   11
    Settling for nothing but the best

Just Ask   19
    Talking and listening to God

Where There's a W.I.L.L., There's a Way   27
    Reading and understanding God's written instructions

Good Advice   37
    Adults do know something! Just ask

Check it Out!   45
    Becoming a student of life

Just Do It!   55
    Don't put off till tomorrow what God wants you to do today

READY FOR LIFE

Contributors

Karen Dockrey has served two churches as minister of youth. She currently spends her professional time writing for youth and their leaders. Karen is the author of over fifteen books, including *The Holman Student Bible Dictionary* (Holman) and *The Youth Worker's Guide to Creative Bible Study* (Victor Books). She earned her M.Div. from Southern Baptist Theological Seminary and currently works with youth at Bluegrass Baptist Church in Hendersonville, Tennessee.

Kevin Johnson is the Associate Pastor for Junior High at Elmbrook Church in Waukesha, Wisconsin. He is the author of the junior high devotionals, *Can I Be a Christian Without Being Weird* (Bethany House) and *Why is God Looking for Friends?* (Bethany House). Kevin received his B.A. in English and Print Journalism from University of Wisconsin/River Falls, and his M.Div. from Fuller Theological Seminary.

Bob Krafft is the Campus Life/JV coordinator for Northwest Indiana Youth for Christ in Auburn, Indiana. He has written training and curriculum materials for Youth for Christ/USA and serves as the national Campus Life/JV director for YFC/USA. Bob has his bachelor degrees in Bible and in Business Administration from Fort Wayne Bible College.

Greg Lafferty is pastor to Junior High students at Saddleback Valley Community Church in Mission Viejo, California. He was most recently Pastor to Junior Highers at Wheaton Bible Church in Wheaton, Illinois for several years. Previously, he wrote junior high Sunday School materials for Scripture Press. Greg graduated from Wheaton College in 1984 with a B.A. in Christian Education.

Tom Nummela is editor, writer, and director of Christian Education in the Lutheran Church (Missouri Synod). He has written Sunday School material for junior high-aged young people and preteens, and currently, he is editing high school Bible study materials. Tom earned his B.A. in Arts and Music and his Lutheran Director of Christian Education Certificate from Concordia College (Seward, Nebraska). He also received his Master of Church Music degree from Concordia University (River Forest, Illinois).

Mark Oestreicher is Junior High Pastor at Lake Avenue Congregational Church in Pasadena, California and has been a pastor of young teens for over seven years. He has written or contributed to over 10 books, including *Flex Sessions* (Victor Books). In addition, Mark has published articles in six magazines. Previously, he was a young teen curriculum editor at Scripture Press. Mark earned his B.A. in Christian Education from Wheaton College, Wheaton, Illinois and his M.A. in Educational Ministries from Wheaton Graduate School.

Ginny Olson serves as Assistant Director of Sunlight Express, the Junior High ministry of Willow Creek Community Church in South Barrington, Illinois. She also serves as Editor of *Journey*, a newsletter for women in youth ministry. Ginny received her B.A. in Biblical and Theological Studies from Bethel College, St. Paul, Minnesota, and her M.A. in Educational Ministries from Wheaton Graduate School, Wheaton, Illinois.

Editor

Dave Veerman worked for 26 years for Youth for Christ, and currently is Vice President and Partner in The Livingstone Corporation. For the past several years, he has worked with junior highers at the Naperville Presbyterian Church in Naperville, Illinois and at Hill Middle School through Campus Life/JV. Dave has authored more than 25 books, including *Youth Evangelism* (Victor Books), *Reaching Kids Before High School* (Victor Books), *Small Group Ministry with Youth* (Victor Books), *Video Movies Worth Watching* (Baker Book House), and *How to Apply the Bible* (Tyndale House). He also served as the General Editor for the *Life Application Bible for Students* (Tyndale House). Dave has his B.A. in Bible from Wheaton College and his M.Div. from Trinity Evangelical Divinity School.

WELCOME TO *READY FOR LIFE!*

These meetings are designed to teach junior high students biblically-based life skills. Early adolescents face dramatic changes physically, socially, spiritually, mentally, and emotionally. Life can be confusing as they transform from children into young adults. During this time, they are learning much about themselves and the world. And they are dealing with the strong desire to feel competent—to be good at something. In other words, they want to learn skills, the "how to's." That's why kids this age will sign up for lessons, clinics, camps, and teams for sports, music, and other skills-based activities. At the same time, they are facing the challenges of "growing up." In other words, they now have a whole set of life skills that they need to learn in order to function well in society. These skills range from knowing how to relate to the opposite sex to knowing how to communicate with adults.

With such a strong emphasis on competence, it only makes sense that curriculum and other materials designed for this age group emphasize the teaching of skills. That's why we created *Ready for Life*. Each book in this series contains six meetings focusing on a specific life skill, a skill needed by junior highers as they grow and mature. By definition, a skill is a "how to." So learning a skill means learning "how to" do something. Thus, each of the life skills in *Ready for Life* will begin with those important words . . . how to.

Four basic steps are necessary in teaching *any* skill: explanation (in which the teacher explains the skill), demonstration (in which the teacher demonstrates the skill), supervision (in which students practice the skill under the watchful eye of the teacher), and implementation (in which students practice the skill on their own). In *Ready for Life*, these skill-teaching steps are found in the following sections of each meeting: BIBLE SEARCH (explanation), DEMONSTRATION (demonstration), PRACTICE (supervision), and ASSIGNMENT (implementation).

As we wrote these meetings, we also kept in mind other characteristics of early adolescents, including their short attention span and their tendency to think in concrete terms. Therefore, each meeting is designed to be *fun, creative, fast-moving, concrete,* and *practical*. In addition, these meetings center on the Bible; that is, the life skill being taught flows from a principle of Scripture—these are Christian and biblical life skills.

Another important rule we followed as we designed and wrote is that the meetings had to be volunteer-friendly. All the recommended props and other materials are cheap and easy to find, and no meeting requires expensive or sophisticated equipment. And every page includes plenty of space for you to write your own thoughts, adaptations, and plans. Go ahead—write in the book!

Each meeting is divided into the following parts:

Objective—the desired result of the meeting; the part of the life skill being taught

Materials Needed—the props and other materials that the leader-teacher should gather before the meeting

Opener—an opening game, tied to the theme of the meeting, designed to be fun and to get all the kids involved (about 5 minutes)

Review—an activity or discussion that reviews the content and the assignment from the previous meeting (2-3 minutes)

Starter—a game that introduces the topic of the meeting and gets kids thinking, talking about, and feeling the need for learning the skill (about 5 minutes)

Bible Search—a close look at Scripture—through discussion, small groups, worksheets, or short talks—to discover the life skill (7-10 minutes)

Demonstration—a demonstration by the leader-teacher of how the skill works, using role plays, case studies, and personal stories (7-10 minutes)

Practice—supervised practice by students of the life skill just explained and demonstrated (7-10 minutes)

Assignment—a specific task for students to do on their own during the week to help them implement the life skill (2-3 minutes)

Surprise—an activity, game, or treat to end the meeting with fun and excitement (about 5 minutes)

We have also included **Extras**, other ideas for enhancing the teaching and fun of the meeting. Each meeting takes about 45 minutes, but can be expanded by adding Extras.

I must also add that the creators and writers of *Ready for Life* are highly qualified men and women, from a wide range of church backgrounds, geography, and personal experience. They know kids; they know what they are talking about; and they know youth ministry. Check out their credentials on the previous pages.

Having said that, remember that only *you* know *your* group of students. All the activities in this book should work well with most junior highers, but even the best of them will not necessarily always work with all students. Feel free to adapt this material to suit the unique needs of your group. Again, only you know your kids—trust your judgment.

Well, that's about all I can think to tell you about this series. I pray that God will use these materials to help you reach kids and help you prepare them to be *Ready for Life*.

Dave Veerman, Series Editor

P.S. Check out *Reaching Kids Before High School* (Victor Books). I think you will find it to be a valuable resource.

HOW TO KNOW WHAT GOD WANTS— MEETING ONE

ONLY THE BEST

OBJECTIVE
As a result of this meeting, students will know that God's way is best.

MATERIALS
- [ ] Bibles
- [ ] Marker board or chalkboard and markers/chalk (OPENER)
- [ ] Blindfolds (two to four) (OPENER)
- [ ] Paper and pencils (DISCUSSION STARTER)
- [ ] Small prize (DISCUSSION STARTER)

Settling for nothing but the best

OPENER
Blind Leading the Blind

Blindfold a few pairs of students and assign them difficult tasks to complete, such as exchanging shoes and socks, doing a difficult math problem on the board, or locating a group member and singing happy birthday. You may want to spin the pair around and make them find the blackboard and write their names on it too. Have the rest of the group act as spotters as your blindfolded students navigate the room. Afterward, congratulate the participants on finding their way under very difficult circumstances.

DISCUSSION STARTER
Idiot Test

Distribute sheets of paper and pencils. Have everyone number their sheets from one to fifteen. Tell them to answer *a, b, c,* or *d* to each question. Then, instead of actually asking questions, simply say: **Number one. What is the correct answer?** Do this with each number and allow time for them to write an answer. If students complain that the test is unfair or impossible, tell them to be quiet. Act as if they should know the answers. Score the test according to a random key you have prepared beforehand and award a small prize to the person with the most correct answers.

BIBLE SEARCH
Follow the Instructions

If you are still alive after administering the Idiot Test, ask the group what they thought of it. Was it fair? What could they have done to perform better?

Blind Leading the Blind
5 MINUTES

Idiot Test
5 MINUTES

Follow the Instructions
7 MINUTES

Then ask them what they thought of the opening game, Blind Leading the Blind. Why did the blindfolded students have a difficult time following the instructions and completing the task?

Say something like: **A lot of us feel as though obeying God is just like the Idiot Test or the Blind Leading the Blind—that it's difficult to figure out the instructions and almost impossible to complete the task. We also may think that what God wants us to do is stupid or senseless.** *Perhaps God is just being mean,* **we think.**

Yet God is good, and the only way we'll follow Him is if we have *confidence* **that God is good and wants what's best for us.**

Have a student read Jeremiah 29:11 aloud. Ask: **What does this passage say about God's will for us?** Discuss briefly. (God has good plans for us.)

Then ask: **How do people figure out what's good and bad and what's right and wrong?** Write their answers on the board. Answers might include: asking friends, parents, and teachers; thinking it through; going with one's feelings; reading the Bible; using occult and New Age techniques. Explain that some of those things can be helpful to us, and some can lead us astray. But the one thing we can be sure of is that what God wants is the smartest, kindest, and best plan for us. None of His directions are dumb. All of His directions are for our good.

DEMONSTRATION
Forced Choice

Forced Choice
8 MINUTES

Have everyone stand in the middle of the room. Tell them that you are about to give them either/or choices in describing a teacher at school. The idea is that they should choose what kind of teacher they'd rather have. They'll demonstrate their choice by going to the appropriate side of the room.

Practice with this example: I like Coke (to left side of the room) or I like Pepsi (to the right side of the room.) Make sure everyone moves to either one side or the other (no abstentions or fence-sitting allowed).

Then, begin the real exercise. Precede each forced choice with: **Who would you rather have as a teacher at school . . .** and then read the two-sided option. Make sure everyone goes to one side of the room or the other. To keep students honest, occasionally ask one or two students to defend their choice. Between each choice, read the statement about God's character and the accompanying verse. Have the verses marked ahead of time to eliminate flipping pages during the activity.

Here are the choices: **Who would you rather have as a teacher at school:**

- a stranger or someone who knows you inside out?

  God knows us better than anyone else (Psalm 139:1-4)

- someone strong or a weakling?

  God is all-powerful (Job 42:2)

- someone who makes you do everything yourself or someone who helps you?

  God gives us strength (Philippians 4:13)

- someone who gives you second chances or someone who never lets you live down a mistake?

  God forgives (1 John 1:9)

- a liar or someone who always tells the truth?

  God never lies (Hebrews 6:18)

- someone who wants what's best for you or someone who is selfish?

  God wants what's best (Jeremiah 29:11)

Demonstration
Continued

- someone who makes fun of you or someone who understands you?

  God understands our struggles and sympathizes with us (Hebrews 4:15)

- someone giving or someone stingy?

  God gives freely (Psalm 84:11)

- a grouch or a nice person?

  God is kind to us (Psalm 86:15)

- someone who talks clearly or someone who mumbles?

  God speaks clearly (Psalm 119:105)

- someone who is never there when you need him or someone who is always available?

  God never leaves us (Hebrews 13:5b)

When you are finished, explain that most of the choices were pretty obvious—we would rather have a teacher with good qualities than one who's not on our side. God has nothing but the best qualities, and He wants what's best for us. That means God is worth trusting!

PRACTICE
Discussion

Discussion
10 MINUTES

Break into groups of ten or fewer, each with an adult leader. (If you don't have any other adult leaders, stay together in one large group.) Have them discuss two questions:

- Of all the things you know God wants you to do or not do, which is the most difficult to do or not do? Why?

- How can we know that doing God's will is best for us?

If your group has a difficult time coming up with specific commands they find difficult to follow, have them look at the Ten Commandments in Exodus 20 and ask:

- **Which commandments are the toughest to keep?**
- **Why does God give us rules?**
- **What reasons does God have for each of the commands?**

ASSIGNMENT
Ask a Friend

Tell students that during the week, they each should ask a friend who doesn't go to church whether he or she thinks God wants what's best for us. Because that's a bold question for junior high age students to ask, promise to do the same with a non-Christian friend or coworker.

Ask a Friend
5 MINUTES

SURPRISE
Sing a Song

Sing a song about doing God's will, or lead your group in singing *Godzwilla* to the tune of *Amazing Grace*:

Sing a Song
5 MINUTES

Godzwilla
Some people think that God is mean.
They think He's big and green.
Godzwilla from the movie screen
Is who they think they've seen.
Through pray'r, God's Word, and godly friends
He shows me how to live.
Godzwilla's not the God I serve.
The God I trust and love.

EXTRA
Write It!

Write a TV or magazine ad persuading people to obey God. The ad can be acted out or drawn from scratch, borrowed from TV, or cut and pasted from magazines.

HOW TO KNOW WHAT GOD WANTS—MEETING TWO

JUST ASK

OBJECTIVE
As a result of this meeting students will learn how to ask God to reveal what He wants them to do (in prayer).

MATERIALS
- ☐ Bibles
- ☐ Small candy bars (OPENER)
- ☐ Marker board or chalkboard and markers/chalk (BIBLE SEARCH)
- ☐ Treats/refreshments (SURPRISE)

Talking and listening to God

OPENER
Please, Oh Please!

Ask for a volunteer who would like to earn a candy bar. Explain that it will take a little effort to earn it but that it will only take a minute or two.

Then line up three or four *other* students; they will be Cruel Masters. Explain quietly to the Masters that the first volunteer (the Doggie) will ask them for food, and that they have only three responses: "Get lost!" "Why should I?" and, "Only if you stop bugging me." Only after the third answer can they give the volunteer a small candy bar.

Tell the first volunteer (the Doggie, who doesn't know it yet) that he or she needs to ask for the candy bar by getting on his or her knees, sticking his or her tongue out like a dog, and saying, "Please, oh *please* give me a doggie biscuit!"

After the first request, the Master should answer, "Get lost!" After the second request, the Master should say, "Why should I?" After the third, he or she should answer, "Only if you promise to stop bugging me." After the third request, the first Master should give the Doggie a tiny piece of the candy bar. Repeat the process with the other Masters. The last Master can give the Doggie the rest of the candy bar, and the group can give a round of applause.

REVIEW
Questions

Review what you discussed last week by saying something like: **Last week we talked about how we can be sure that God is good and that when He gives us a rule or direction, it's for our best. Who asked anyone if they thought that God wants the best for us? What did your friends say?** Discuss the students' and leaders' answers.

Please, Oh Please!
5 MINUTES

Questions
3 MINUTES

Cruel Masters
5 MINUTES

DISCUSSION STARTER
Cruel Masters

Ask the group to help you make a list of people they would never ask for help because they're just like the cruel masters in the Opener. Ask them to think about people in their neighborhood, at school, or wherever; list the people they think of using descriptions only (that is, without using names). Some examples: A teacher who thinks that all questions from students are dumb; a store clerk who thinks students are shoplifters just because they're junior highers; a parent who always answers children's questions with, "When I was your age. . ." When you have come up with several examples, point out that if that's what we think God is like, we'll never go to Him to ask for help when we need it. Or we'll give up because we think He's mean.

BIBLE SEARCH
Just Ask

Just Ask
10 MINUTES

Explain that at times in life when we don't know what to do, God does know. And what He thinks is best and right. So whenever we are confused or uncertain about some decision, we should ask Him for wisdom. He promises that He will help us.

Have a student read James 1:5-8 aloud. Ask:

- **How does James 1:5-8 picture God?**
- **What makes God different from the Cruel Master type of person?**

Discuss each question briefly. Then say: **God is the exact opposite of the cruel masters. He never says, "Get lost!" "Why should I?" or "Only if you promise to stop bugging me." God isn't a grouch in the way He gives to us. James 1:5 says that God gives (1) generously and (2) without finding fault. God doesn't put us down for needing help.**

God has expectations of us, though, when we ask. He wants us to believe and not doubt that His way is best. What is the doubter like (James 1:6-8)? The passage uses two illustrations: (1) A wave changes form and can be blown all over the place by the wind; (2) a double-minded person is someone whose brain is going in two directions, not sure whether he wants God's will or his own will.

Explain that we don't like it if someone is two-faced—when someone acts like a friend sometimes and as a stranger or enemy at other times, or someone who says one thing to our face and another behind our back. God doesn't like it when we're like that to Him either. He wants us to be single-minded, to want His will more than anything else. We can have this confidence by trusting—not doubting—that God wants only what's best for us (the topic discussed last week).

To wrap up, introduce the acrostic that will help students remember how to find God's W.I.L.L. Write the "W.I.L.L." vertically on the board. The W stands for *Wait on the Lord*. Explain that because some answers to prayer take months or even years to come about, Christians often talk about prayer and listening to God as "waiting on the Lord."

Explain that you will continue to fill in the other words in the acrostic in following weeks.

DEMONSTRATION
Three Steps

Explain that there are three steps to finding God's will through prayer: (1) *Be confident* about God's goodness that God wants what's best for us and that He is eager to show His will to us. (2) *Be right* with God, not letting any sin or double-mindedness hinder our friendship with Him. (3) *Be ready* to act on what we learn from God, on His terms, not ours.

Three Steps
7 MINUTES

Write the following steps on the board, explain what each means, and discuss the questions:

1. *Be confident about God.* **What can you do if you're not confident?** (Look back at the previous lesson's Scripture references and sources of confidence; realize that God's plans for us are good.)

2. *Be right.* **What should you do if there's something between you and God?** (1 John 1:9—confess sin and turn from it.)

3. *Be ready to act on what you learn.* **What should you do if you're not ready?** (Romans 12:1-2—let God renew your mind.)

PRACTICE
Prayer

Prayer
8 MINUTES

Because this meeting is about prayer, spend time praying for each other. Pray for general requests, or specifically about situations in which students are unclear about God's will, such as knowing right from wrong behavior; how to be a Christian at school without losing all your friends; how to show Christ to teachers; how to live with non-Christian parents; or how to get along better with brothers, sisters, and parents.

ASSIGNMENT
Has God Shown You His Will?

Has God Shown You His Will?
2 MINUTES

Have everyone try to think of a situation or a dilemma they face in which they aren't sure of God's will. During the week, they should pray for God to show them His will. At the next meeting, they should be prepared to share their situations and answers to prayer.

SURPRISE
You Don't Have to Beg

Have treats or refreshments ready for the group. Remind students that when we ask God for wisdom, we don't have to beg. To demonstrate that God isn't like the Cruel Masters in the opener, tell students that to get a treat all they have to do is ask. Each person simply needs to say, "May I please have a Ninja Juju Pepper?" (or whatever candy you've brought). The leader(s) passing out the refreshments should respond, "I would be happy to give you a Ninja Juju Pepper" (or whatever) and give the student a treat.

EXTRA
Cheer

Have the group or individuals make up a cheer or a military marching ditty about being confident, right, and/or ready. Have them perform their cheers one individual or group at a time.

You Don't Have to Beg
5 MINUTES

HOW TO KNOW WHAT GOD WANTS—
MEETING THREE

WHERE THERE'S A W.I.L.L., THERE'S A WAY

OBJECTIVE
As a result of this meeting, students will learn how to read the Bible to discover what God wants them to do.

MATERIALS
- [ ] Bibles
- [ ] Chalkboard and chalk (REVIEW)
- [ ] Verse words on miniature candy bars (OPENER)
- [ ] Trays (OPENER)
- [ ] Tape (OPENER)
- [ ] Prize (DISCUSSION STARTER)
- [ ] Verses on slips of paper (PRACTICE)
- [ ] Pencils (ASSIGNMENT)
- [ ] Index cards (ASSIGNMENT)
- [ ] Weird headlines (SURPRISE)

Reading and understanding God's written instructions

OPENER
Verse Scramble Relay

Before the meeting, write single words from Scripture verses on pieces of paper and tape them to miniature candy bars. Keep each verse's bars in its own bag, and have one bag for every four to ten students, depending on how many students you need on each team to form three or more teams.

As the students come into the room, divide them into teams (try to have at least three). Use whatever number makes sense for your group and available space. When you're ready to begin, start the race. Each team should send a representative to the front, who grabs a candy bar from his or her team's bag, runs back, and places it in order on a tray. The first team to figure out their verse is the winner. Suggested verses to use include: Psalm 119:8, Psalm 119:11, Psalm 119:33, and Psalm 119:105.

Afterward, let the teams eat their candy bars.

REVIEW
W

Write W.I.L.L. vertically down the left side of the board and ask someone to tell you what the **W** stands for (from last week's lesson—it stands for *Wait on the Lord*). Then ask for volunteers to share their specific situations where they weren't sure about God's will and prayed about it. Let students know that you are going to deal with those situations a little later in the meeting. Then explain that the second part of learning God's will is to *inquire* into His Word—write "nquire" next to the I in W.I.L.L. Explain that they will be digging in God's Word.

Verse Scramble Relay
5 MINUTES

W
3 MINUTES

Bible Scavenger Hunt
5 MINUTES

DISCUSSION STARTER
Bible Scavenger Hunt

Keep students in the same teams and give Bibles to each team. Explain that when you name an item, they are to race to see who can find a mention of that item in the Bible first. Give points for each item, and give the winning group a treat or prize.

Items to search for:

- An animal
- A Bible book whose name starts with Z
- The name of any city
- The word "wheel"
- A food
- The name of a King
- The word "will"
- A country
- A verb
- A musical instrument
- A weapon
- A woman's name

BIBLE SEARCH
Owner's Manual

Owner's Manual
10 MINUTES

Say something like: **You may wonder how you can look into the Bible to discover God's plan for your life. Let's look at one verse to see how.**

Write out 2 Timothy 3:16 on the board. Then ask the following questions, allowing time for discussion of each.

- **What does the phrase, "All scripture is God-breathed" mean?** (God inspired the writing of the Bible; the message is His message.)

- **We all know what teaching is. But what is *rebuking*?** (Telling someone when he or she is wrong, much the same as correcting, which is to put someone back on the right track. "Training in righteousness" is a little different. Instead of waiting until you mess up, you can read the Bible and know what you should do—God's Will—before things go wrong.)

Explain that the Bible is like a repair manual and maintenance manual all in one. That is, it tells you how to fix the car when it breaks *and also* what to do to keep the car from breaking down in the first place.

Say something like: **While the Bible doesn't give specific answers to all our questions (such as whom to marry or where to work), it *does* tell you how to make these decisions for yourself. Though a car's operating manual won't tell you where your next near collision will occur, it *does* tell you how to steer a car during a skid or how to apply the brakes in an emergency. The manual may not tell you where those events will happen, but at least you'll know what to do when they do.**

Read and discuss the next three passages to illustrate this principle of the Bible giving us general guidelines for our specific circumstances.

Have a student read 1 Corinthians 10:12-13 aloud. Ask: **According to these verses, what emergency procedure does God give direction on?** (Temptation—watch out for it and look for God's way of escape.) **When does this instruction apply to us?** (Actually, all the time, since we should always be on guard. But it also tells us specifically what to do whenever we're tempted.)

Next, have a student read Matthew 5:11-12. Ask: **What emergency procedure do you see in these verses?** (What to do when you're persecuted because of your faith in Christ—be glad.) **When does this instruction apply?** (Whenever we're hassled because of our faith.)

Bible Search
Continued

Finally, have a student read Philippians 2:3-4. Ask: **This passage really isn't for emergencies, but is our normal operating procedure. How does it tell us to live?** (We should be humble and think of others more than ourselves.) **When would this apply?** (Whenever we're feeling conceited or selfish.)

To summarize, explain that those are examples of how the Bible gives us general instructions or directions. Of course, we still have to put them into practice in our lives, but they prepare us to face many situations of life.

DEMONSTRATION
Here's What They Did

Here's What They Did
5 MINUTES

Next, read the following case studies showing how students applied 1 Corinthians 10:12-13, Matthew 5:11-12, and Philippians 2:3-4 to specific life situations.

Aaron

Aaron had been reading in 1 Corinthians for his quiet time. When he read 1 Corinthians 10:12-13, he saw that it was an important instruction, so he underlined it in his Bible. The next day, at school, he was tempted to cheat on a test. Remembering the passage, Aaron looked away from his friend's test and silently prayed for God's way of escape. Just then, the teacher came back into the room.

Maxine

In Sunday School last Sunday, Maxine's class was studying the Sermon on the Mount in Matthew 5. She was especially hit by verses 11 and 12 about how to react when persecuted. The next day, a friend made a joke about the fact that she was a strong Christian. Instead of being angry or sad, Maxine remembered the verses and thanked God for being her friend and for being close to her.

Phil

After dinner last week, Phil's dad read Philippians 2:3-8 to the family, and they discussed the passage. Yesterday, Phil was praised by a teacher for his science project. Remembering the Bible's teaching about being humble, Phil politely thanked the teacher and explained how Jason, his science partner, had done a lot of the work.

PRACTICE
Do It Yourself

Give each student a different verse to look up. (You may want to have these on individual slips of paper and have students draw them from a bag.) Tell them to read the passage and determine God's instruction. Here are some verses to use (you can add others):

- **Matthew 6:33-34** (don't worry)
- **Matthew 18:15** (help a fellow Christian who sins)
- **Mark 10:13-14** (help little children come to Christ)
- **Luke 7:47-48** (Jesus forgives our sins)
- **John 13:12-17** (we should lovingly serve others)
- **Acts 13:46** (speak boldly for Christ)
- **Romans 12:2** (resist peer pressure)
- **1 Corinthians 10:24** (seek the good of others)
- **2 Corinthians 8:7** (be generous)
- **Galatians 5:22** (let God produce these qualities in you)

Do It Yourself
10 MINUTES

- **Ephesians 5:15-16** (be careful how you live)
- **Philippians 4:8** (watch your thoughts)
- **Colossians 2:7** (be thankful)
- **1 Thessalonians 5:15** (be kind)
- **2 Thessalonians 3:1** (pray for Christian workers)

Ask for volunteers to read their verses aloud and then share what they found. Then have everyone think of when their verses and God's directions might be put into practice in their lives. Again have volunteers share their thoughts and ideas.

Digging In
2 MINUTES

ASSIGNMENT
Digging In

Hand out index cards and pencils and have students identify the one or two biggest questions they have about their lives and God's will. (They can use the same questions they came up with last week.) Have them look for verses that might help them with these areas. Encourage them to ask Mom, Dad, a pastor, or another church leader, or to look through topical Bibles. If you have time you may want to give some ideas about where to look before they leave.

Inquiring Minds Want to Know
5 MINUTES

SURPRISE
Inquiring Minds Want to Know

Gather some weird headlines from tabloid magazines and create some wild ones of your own. Divide into groups of ten to fifteen. Put the list on the board and have groups try to identify which ones are fake. Have the groups go in turn, giving you just one guess. If they guess correctly, award them 500 points. If they guess incorrectly, subtract 100 points.

Here are some fake headlines to get you started (you can add others):

- Husband and Wife Surgically Attached at the Hip (He Wanted to Always Be at Her Side)
- Man with Baboon Heart Acts Like Monkey
- Woman Loses Arm in Bank Drive-up Window
- Elvis Stamp Sings "Return to Sender"
- Real Life "Encino Man" Discovered in Juneau
- Michael Jackson's Nose Is Falling Off

EXTRA
A Light on My Foot

Have someone come in and sing or play the song, "Thy Word." Let students sing along. Then have them talk about the meaning of the song.

HOW TO KNOW WHAT GOD WANTS—MEETING FOUR

GOOD ADVICE

OBJECTIVE
As a result of this meeting, students will learn how to listen to the advice of mature Christians in seeking God's will.

MATERIALS
- ☐ Bibles
- ☐ Marker board or chalk board and markers/chalk (REVIEW)
- ☐ Pens/pencils (DISCUSSION STARTER)
- ☐ Index cards (DISCUSSION STARTER)
- ☐ Refreshments or treats (SURPRISE)
- ☐ Marshmallows and small plastic bags (EXTRA)

Adults do know something! Just ask

OPENER
Tell Me What to Do

Have students get into circles of ten to fifteen. Starting with the oldest person, they should tell the person to their right to do an unusual action. That person must do it and then tell the next person to do the same action plus a new one. The rules:

1. They have to stay seated
2. The actions can't be anything gross

Here are some sample actions:

- Stick out your tongue
- Scratch your head
- Blink your eyes
- Touch your nose
- Pull on your ear
- Flap your arms
- Rub your belly
- Pat your head
- Wiggle your nose
- Cry like a baby
- Hum a song
- Stomp your feet
- Hold one foot up
- Shrug your shoulders

REVIEW
W.I.

Have students report on how successful they were at finding Scriptures for their questions about what God wants (last week's assignment). Ask how many of them talked to parents, pastors, or other church lead-

---

Tell Me What to Do
5 MINUTES

W.I.
3 MINUTES

ers for help. Then let them know that talking to mature Christians is exactly the next step to finding out God's will.

Write the word W.I.L.L. vertically down the left side of the board, and have students come up and fill in the W and I (*Wait on the Lord,* and *Inquire into His Word*). Then invite other students to explain each point.

DISCUSSION STARTER
Dear Flabby

Dear Flabby
5 MINUTES

Hand out index cards and pens/pencils to everyone. Tell half the crowd to write brief questions to the World Famous Advice Columnist, Flabigail Van Boring. Encourage them to use their imagination and creativity. At the same time, have the other half of the crowd write Flabigail's answers—that is, *before* they know the questions. Encourage them to use their imagination and creativity too. Also, have any volunteers or adult leaders write questions and answers.

After a few minutes, collect the cards, keeping the questions and answers separate. Then have a leader read the questions one at a time, followed by one of the answers.

Afterward, explain that people look to many different sources for advice. Then explain that the first L in W.I.L.L. stands for *Listening to the advice of mature Christians.* Write "isten" after the first L in W.I.L.L., spelling "Listen."

BIBLE SEARCH
Why Didn't You Ask?

Why Didn't You Ask?
7 MINUTES

Have a student read Proverbs 15:22 aloud. Ask how many of your students have failed at something they did on their own without advice. Ask them:

- **What happened?**
- **Why didn't you ask for advice or help first?** (Afraid that asking might look dumb; too proud.) Usually it's fear more than pride.

Explain that often we fail to ask for advice because we're afraid to . . . only to have someone say, "Why didn't you ask me—I would have helped you out!" Share an example from your own life.

Then explain that as Proverbs 15:22 says, a lot of mistakes happen *because we don't ask for help*. We may be too proud to ask, but usually we are just afraid that asking might look dumb.

Share or have another leader share an example of when asking for advice saved a lot of grief. Maybe it was asking parents, a pastor, or a grandparent for help.

DEMONSTRATION
Who and How

Say something like: **The two words you need to remember when asking for advice are *Who* and *How*. Before you can ask anyone for advice, you have to ask yourself:**

1. **Whom should I ask?**
2. **How should I ask the person?**

For instance, if you need advice on how to fix your car, would you ask a mailman, a first grader, or an auto mechanic? You would probably go to a mechanic. The same is true for problems you have about learning God's will. Should you ask an atheist, a Hindu, or a mature Christian? Obviously, you should ask a mature Christian (preferably someone who's more mature than you are) who has already been through something similar to what you are experiencing.

Who and How
8 MINUTES

The second important word to remember is *How*; in other words, knowing *how* to ask.

Have a student come up and pretend that he or she is a pastor or church leader whom everyone knows. Then do a role play in which you are the young person asking for advice. First, do everything wrong—mumble, stay far enough away that the person can't hear you, avoid eye-contact, be rude, don't give the person a chance to answer, etc. Then have students tell you what you did wrong. When that analysis is complete, role play the situation again, doing everything right.

Afterward, explain these keys to doing it right:

H — *H*ave guts—Look the person in the eye and speak up

O — Be *O*pen to whatever the person says—don't expect the answer you want

W — Ask *W*ith politeness—be sure to say "thank you"

PRACTICE
Ask Me! Ask Me!

- Have students form pairs so they can practice asking for advice from each other. Set them up with a typical, nonthreatening situation—a circumstance in which a student would need help (some samples follow). One part of the pair should play the role of the student asking for advice, and the other that of an advice-giver (let them decide what kind of advice-giver it is—pastor, parent, older Christian, etc.). Remind them of the key things to remember when asking for advice (the HOW acrostic above).

- After a few minutes, give another situation and have students switch roles.

Ask Me! Ask Me!
10 MINUTES

Sample Situations

- You're having problems getting along with your parents.
- Your best friend isn't a Christian and you're concerned for him or her.
- Your friend is using you to cheat on tests at school.
- You wonder what God wants you to do with your life.
- You need help deciding which of your divorced parents to live with.

ASSIGNMENT
Ask Someone

Have students pull out the cards from last week with the questions and problems written on them (or think of new ones). Then have them think of at least one person they can ask for advice. Their assignment is to talk to that person about the problem sometime this week.

SURPRISE
Advice Scavenger Hunt

As preparation for this activity, hide treats or the refreshments somewhere in the building. Also have some adults or volunteers agree to act as advice givers, and give each person one of the roles described in the following paragraph.

Here's the activity. Have the students go out in pairs. They should say, "We need help. Can you tell us what to do?" to the first advice-giver outside the door. This advice-giver should then give the students vague advice to take a certain route, where they will find an-

Ask Someone
2 MINUTES

Advice Scavenger Hunt
5 MINUTES

> **Surprise**
> *Continued*

other advice-giver whom he or she vaguely describes.

When that pair is gone, let the next pair go out and ask for help. (This will take some time to plan—think through your facility and who you have available to be advice givers.)

EXTRA
Mr. Mumbles

Using competing pairs, give each pair a small plastic bag of marshmallows (no more than six in each bag). Have each pair designate a Talker and a Listener. Explain that you will give each Talker a phrase to communicate to his or her Listener. He or she should put a marshmallow in his or her mouth and then read the phrase off the card you hold up. Immediately following, his or her partner (the Listener) should repeat the phrase for the entire group to hear. With each phrase, the Talker should add a marshmallow (without swallowing it). Pairs are eliminated from competition if the Listeners cannot understand the phrases being communicated. Congratulate them if they get through six marshmallows successfully.

Here are some possible phrases to use:

- I love to eat.
- You are very special!
- Let's go out for pizza afterward.
- Who are you voting for in the next election?
- I'm really upset about the way things are going in this country.
- Vertical latitude is exponentially rectified by parallel hypothermia.
- (Add others)

HOW TO KNOW WHAT GOD WANTS—MEETING FIVE

CHECK IT OUT!

OBJECTIVE
As a result of this meeting, students will learn how to assess circumstances.

MATERIALS
- [ ] Bibles
- [ ] Balloons (OPENER)
- [ ] Marker board or chalkboard and markers/chalk (REVIEW)
- [ ] Masking tape (DISCUSSION STARTER, ASSIGNMENT, SURPRISE)
- [ ] Blue and brown construction paper (DISCUSSION STARTER)
- [ ] Blindfold (DISCUSSION STARTER)
- [ ] Poster with traffic signal on it (BIBLE SEARCH)
- [ ] Red, yellow, and green circles three to five inches across (DEMONSTRATION)
- [ ] Scissors and red, yellow, and green string or craft cord and red, yellow, and green beads (ASSIGNMENT, SURPRISE)
- [ ] Refreshments (SURPRISE)

Becoming a student of life

Check it Out!

PREPARATION

For Opener, you will need six to twelve balloons, blown up to about ten or twelve inches across.

For Discussion Starter, you will need a medium sized brown paper bag, masking tape, and some blue and brown construction paper or poster board. If possible, lay out the course described below in advance.

Have extra Bibles ready for the Bible Search. A poster board or newsprint page made to look like a stop-light would be a helpful visual aid for this part.

During Demonstration, sharing might be easier for the students if you have a set of red, yellow, and green circles (cut from poster board or other substantial material) three to five inches across. These will be passed around the sharing circle.

For Assignment and Surprise, you may want to have each participant make a power bracelet or friendship bracelet. For the power bracelet, you will need about nine inches of craft cord or thin leather thong and three beads (red, yellow, and green) for each participant. For friendship bracelets, bring red, yellow, and green string. Scissors and masking tape should also be available.

OPENER
Heads Up!

Arrange the group into circles of six to eight students each (you will need at least two circles). Give each team (circle) an inflated balloon. At the word "Go," someone should toss the balloon in the air, and from then on the team must be kept it airborne using only their *heads*—no hands, arms, knees, or other body parts allowed. Each round lasts until only one team still has their balloon aloft. They win that round. If things go quickly, play several rounds.

Heads Up!
5 MINUTES

W.I.L.
3 MINUTES

Afterward, congratulate the winners with a cheer and round of applause for *using their heads*.

REVIEW
W.I.L.

Ask who did the assignment from the last meeting. (The assignment was to ask someone for advice about an important question.) Ask volunteers to share their experiences.

Write W.I.L.L. vertically down the left side of the board and see if students can fill in the words for the first three letters (*Wait on the Lord, Inquire into His Word,* and *Listen to advice from mature Christians*). Then have them guess what the last L might stand for. After they've guessed a few times, let them know that it means "**Look at your circumstances.**" Write this on the board after the last L.

DISCUSSION STARTER
Lose Your Head

Lose Your Head
5 MINUTES

Prepare a simple course in your meeting room using masking tape and blue and brown paper. The course should consist of a winding path about 50 feet long with "water hazards" and "mud holes" (areas where blue and brown paper lie on the ground) on either side of the path. Ask for three volunteers (preferably two guys and a girl or two girls and a guy) who are willing to try the course.

Before they begin, explain that one of the volunteers has "lost his (or her) head." Then place a brown paper bag over the participant's head and fold the front edge of the bag under the person's chin so that he or she can't peek at the ground. (If that doesn't work, use a blindfold.)

Inform the "headless" participant that the other two volunteers will be giving instructions to follow the track, but with one hitch—one of them will be giving bogus instructions, the other real. Explain that if the person listens carefully, he or she may be able to discern the truth. Whisper to one of the remaining volunteers that their task is to get the "headless" one *off track* with wrong instructions; whisper to the other one that he or she is to keep the "headless" one *on track* if possible. Tell the rest of the group to keep silent as they watch. As things progress, shout out when the "headless" one gets into a water hazard or a mud hole; if necessary, help the person get back on track. Stop when the person gets to the end of the course or gets hopelessly lost.

If things go quickly, choose another set of volunteers. After a few minutes, debrief the experience with questions such as these:

- **How did it feel to "have no head?"**
- **How did you decide whom to listen to?**
- **What would you do differently if you played the game again?**

Reclaim your paper bag or blindfold, ask the volunteers to be seated with the group, and continue with Bible Search.

BIBLE SEARCH
Red Lights and Green Lights

Display a poster or picture of a Traffic Signal and start with this story (it may be familiar, but it quickly makes the point):

There was a man caught on his roof during a flood. A neighbor came by in a row boat to rescue the man, but he answered: "No not yet, I've prayed to God and I'm sure he'll rescue me." As the

---

Red Lights and Green Lights
8 MINUTES

Bible Search
Continued

water got higher, a rescue team came in a power boat, but the man refused to go, saying, "I'm sure God has heard my prayers; He'll rescue me." As the water began to lap over the sides of the roof to which the man clung, a helicopter hovered overhead, offering to let down a line and carry the man to safety. But he confidently replied, "No need! God will rescue me any minute now!" The water soon covered the house, washed the man away, and he drowned.

When the man discovered he was in heaven, he demanded to see God. "God, I prayed to you continuously! How could you just let me drown?"

God replied, "After you ignored both of my boats and my helicopter, you should be glad you're here at all!"

After the story, continue: **Scripture is filled with examples of God-given opportunities that people missed. God has given us the ability to analyze the circumstances around us and to make wise decisions. In other words, He also asks us to use our heads.**

A Missed Red Light
Have everyone look up Luke 10:30-37 and follow along as volunteers read the verses aloud. Explain that some people in this story missed a "red light" from God. Discuss:

- **Who missed God's red light?** (The priest and Levite)
- **Why did they miss what God wanted them to do?** (They were caught up in their sense of importance and responsibility; they didn't want to be interrupted.)
- **What were the priest and Levite lacking?** (Perhaps a sense of responsibility, a conscience, and/or a willingness to do what was right.)

A Green Light (after several red ones)

Next, tell everyone to look at Acts 16:6-8, a little episode in Paul's second missionary journey. While they read, quickly sketch on the board a map of the region involved (most Bibles have one in the back if you don't have any other sources). Label Troas (center), Macedonia (left), Galatia (right), Bithynia (above Galatia), and Asia (below Troas). Be ready to draw a line from the right side of the board to Troas, showing that Paul was not "allowed" to go south to Asia or north to Bithynia.

Then discuss:

- **What kept Paul from going anywhere but Troas?** (The Holy Spirit—we don't know if it was through visions, circumstances, prophesies, or some other means, but God led him.)
- **What led Paul to go to Macedonia?** (A vision from God)

Ask students to mention at least one other "signal light" experience from the Bible. (Some examples include Gideon in Judges 6–7, David in 1 Samuel 23, and Hezekiah in Isaiah 37.)

DEMONSTRATION
Red Light, Green Light

The best demonstration of God's use of circumstances in guiding us would be your own personal testimony. If God has ever used circumstances to guide you, spend some time thinking about the "red lights" and "green lights" that pointed the way. Develop a *brief* talk (no speeches necessary—just the essential facts) based on the following outline:

1. The Straight Path (the direction you were headed)
2. The Signal (the circumstances that God used to redirect you)

> **Red Light, Green Light**
> 7 MINUTES

3. The Results (how your life's path changed)

It might help to write down your thoughts even if you know what you want to say. This will force you to ponder the experience a little longer and may remind you of details you had forgotten.

PRACTICE
Sharing Circles

Sharing Circles
10 MINUTES

Ask the students to gather in circles of about five kids each (plus an adult if possible). Give each circle a set of three small colors (red, yellow, and green). Tell students to pass the three colors around one at a time; when you call out red, the person holding that color should quickly think of any circumstance in which God might send a "red light." (Allow about a half minute). Do the same with the other colors. After each time, tell them to pass the colors again. Do this like musical chairs, with the colors moving until the music stops. The idea is to get students thinking about how God could be seeking to interrupt them in their lives to guide or direct them.

ASSIGNMENT
Power Bracelet

Power Bracelet
2 MINUTES

Tell the group that during the fellowship time and refreshments, each person should make a Power Bracelet (see the illustration on next page) with craft cord and red, yellow, and green beads. (An option would be to make friendship bracelets of red, yellow, and green string.) Challenge them to wear the bracelet all week, using it to remind them to look for circumstances in their lives through which God may be saying, "Stop," "Go," or "Watch Out."

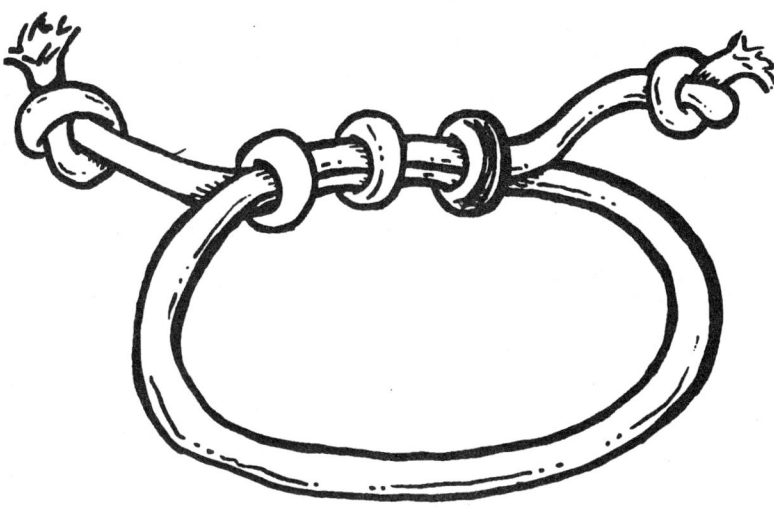

The bracelet can be a powerful reminder that students should continue to pray, study the Bible, and stay in contact with other Christians.

SURPRISE
Make a Reminder

While refreshments are served, help the students make the bracelets described in Assignment. Power Bracelets are made by stringing the beads on a nine inch length of cord (wrapping one end of the cord with masking tape makes this relatively easy), passing one end of the cord through the beads a second time to complete the circle (see the illustration), and knotting both ends.

Place the second knot so that when knots and beads are tightly together, the bracelet can be taken off; when the beads are spread out a little, the bracelet will stay on the wrist.

If you choose to make Friendship Bracelets, someone in the group may know several ways of doing this. The easiest ways is to tie the three strands together with a knot at one end, tape the knot to the surface of a table, and braid the strands, alternately passing

Make a Reminder
5 MINUTES

Surprise
Continued

the side strands over the top of the center one. (See the illustration.) When braided seven to nine inches long, tie the other end and have someone tie it to your wrist.

EXTRAS
Red Light, Green Light

If you have time or need to fill time with another activity, try a round or two of the children's game, "Red Light, Green Light." In this game, a leader on one side of the room turns his or her back away from the others and shouts, "Green Light!" The rest of the group tries to approach the leader but must be completely still the instant the leader shouts "Red Light" and turns back around (in that order). If the leader sees anyone moving when he or she turns around, that person is out or must start over.

For a new wrinkle, have a girl be leader against the guys and a guy be leader against the girls in simultaneous games. See which group tags the leader first.

HOW TO KNOW WHAT GOD WANTS—
MEETING SIX

JUST DO IT!

OBJECTIVE
As a result of this meeting, students will understand that when they know what God wants them to do, they should just do it!

MATERIALS
- [ ] Bibles
- [ ] Marker board or chalkboard and markers/chalk (OPENER)
- [ ] Copies of the "Coin Races" worksheet (OPENER)
- [ ] Pennies, dimes, nickels, and quarters (OPENER)
- [ ] Toothpicks (OPENER)
- [ ] Stopwatch or watch with second hand (OPENER)
- [ ] Case Studies worksheet (DEMONSTRATION/PRACTICE)
- [ ] Refreshments (SURPRISE)

Don't put off till tomorrow what God wants you to do today

OPENER
Coin Races

Prepare enough Coin Race tracks for every four students you expect by photocopying the "Coin Races" worksheet. Have a penny, dime, nickel, and quarter available for each track and toothpicks for each student. The track is a simple winding maze (like a miniature divided road).

Have students line up at each track on a table. Give each a toothpick and a car—one of the four coins. The car should be placed completely behind the starting line. Have a volunteer time the race with a stop watch (or a watch with a second hand). A racer drives his or her car around the track by moving the coin with the toothpick only. His or her score is the number of seconds it takes to get completely over the finish line. Have each person record his or her score on a board in front of the room.

Note: You can use the finish order later as the order for getting refreshments, going in order of fastest time first.

The race has only two rules:

1. Only the toothpick may touch the car during the race except . . .
2. . . . if the car leaves the track or crosses the center line completely, it must be picked up and placed behind the starting line to start over.

Observe the game carefully. Listen for how the students learn to do the task well. Do they ask questions? Listen to instructions? Ask for advice? Learn by trial and error? Do they go slowly and carefully, or do they drive fast?

Coin Races
10 MINUTES

The Race
3 MINUTES

When everyone has had a chance to drive, collect the game pieces and have the students sit down. If you want to wow them, demonstrate the game by breaking your toothpick in half and advancing your car with one half pushing and the other half holding the car firmly to the track. You'll probably beat the best time by half!

REVIEW
The Race

When the group is seated, comment about what you observed. Write W.I.L.L. vertically down the left side of the board and invite the students to recall each of the four steps to finding God's will (taught in the previous sessions—*Wait on the Lord, Inquire into His Word, Listen to advice,* and *Look at your circumstances*). Ask how the Power Bracelets (or Friendship Bracelets) worked as reminders.

DISCUSSION STARTER
A Fishing Story

A Fishing Story
3 MINUTES

Say something like: **I'd like to share a short story with you. I bet you'll be able to tell very quickly how it relates to our topic.**

There once was a guy who was very interested in fishing. He bought the very best fishing equipment. He practiced using it. He wrote to the greatest fishing expert of all time and asked for help.

He read every book he could find about fishing, went to fishing schools, and talked about fishing all the time. He asked all his friends what they knew about fishing and considered their advice.

Sometimes he even went to watch others fish.

But when his friends would call to invite him to go fishing, he never seemed to have time. "Oh, I'm in the middle of the best fishing book I've ever read," he'd say. Or, "I'd love to, but I promised a friend I'd practice casting with him today."

Needless to say, his friends thought him to be very strange. It became apparent that this guy was the most unusual fisherman of all time. He became known as *the fisherman who never fished.*

After telling the story, discuss:

- **What's the point of that story?** (It's one thing to know about something; it's another thing to do it.)
- **How does this relate to our discussions about knowing God's will?** (It is not enough to *know it*—we must also *do it!*)

BIBLE SEARCH
Go Fishing!

Say something like: **Once you've** *waited on God, inquired of Him, listened to the advice of mature Christians,* **and** *looked at your circumstances* **to adjust your sights, what's next? Fishing! That is, make your best decision and go with it!**

Summarize these four points from God's Word:

1. Be open to new experiences. Look at it this way: Would you rather travel with God on a train or a bus? When your journey with God is like a train, it follows a set route—to church and home again, to school and home again, to the mall and home again. That kind of routine can not only get boring, but it also may prevent you from experiencing the new opportunities God has for you.

Acts 10 tells about a time when the Apostle Peter

Go Fishing!
7 MINUTES

was on a Jewish train trip. Like a good Jew, he was unwilling to have anything to do with the Gentiles. But God derailed Peter's train—God showed him that Jesus died for the Gentiles too. Because Peter was open to this, he made the change that God wanted him to make.

2. Remember that God can use what we do better than what we don't do. God called Jonah to a ministry in the foreign city of Nineveh. Jonah didn't just refuse and sit still, he ran the opposite way, toward Spain. And while Jonah was on the move, God steered him into the mouth of the great fish and then back on the road to Nineveh. Through Jonah, the whole city was converted.

3. Remember that God is in control. We may not fully understand God's will; we may not even fully follow it. But remember the words that Joseph spoke to his brothers when he finally had the chance to pay them back for selling him as a slave to Egypt: You intended to harm me, but God intended it all for good (Genesis 50:20).

4. Finally, remember that God's business is forgiving failure. Even when we goof up completely in our efforts to follow God, He stands ready to forgive, strengthen, and support us in our next efforts. No one except Jesus Christ has been able to follow God's will perfectly. Don't let fear of failure stop you from giving things a try.

Summarize by saying something like: **The bottom line is,** *do it.* **Remember Philippians 4:13— "I can do everything through Him who gives me strength"** (NIV).

DEMONSTRATION/PRACTICE
Case Studies

Divide into three groups. Give each group a Case Study worksheet to read and discuss. Explain that they

Case Studies
15 MINUTES

should decide what the person in the case study should do next and why. Afterward, have each group read their case study to the whole group and tell what they decided.

Before the groups begin discussing their Case Studies, tell them to remember the points in the Bible Search. Then, as you discuss each study and what the groups decided, ask which points seemed to apply most to their particular situation.

In debriefing the Case Studies, remember that there are no right or wrong answers. Respect all the opinions that your students express. Compliment those who make use of the process to apply the principles they've learned.

To conclude, ask for suggestions of other, similar situations in the lives of kids their age. Then pray with the students for growth in the ability to know God's will and the courage to trust in His promise—"I can do everything through Him who gives me strength" (Philippians 4:13, NIV).

ASSIGNMENT
Just Do It!

After prayer, quickly review the four W.I.L.L. steps. Urge students to use them and then to JUST DO IT!

SURPRISE
Racing Rewards

Serve refreshments (such as cup cakes). Use the results of the Coin Races to introduce the first place winner and let him or her get the first treat; then second place, etc.

Just Do It!
2 MINUTES

Racing Rewards
5 MINUTES

EXTRA
Yikes, Nikes!

Provide magazines and newspapers. Divide the group into smaller groups of six and give them two minutes to find, tear out, and stack up Nike ads. The group with the most ads wins. Award a simple prize, such as bubble gum. The other groups win clean-up duty.

Ask what the message of the ads is ("Just Do It!") and what it means.

Coin Races

Case Study One

From all the students in your school, you have been recommended to spend a year in a foreign exchange program in Japan. You've prayed about it and see, through your Bible study, that you might have many opportunities to share your faith during that year. You've talked with your pastor and youth leader about your fears and your excitement about the opportunity. Things even seem to be falling into place for the financial support you would need.

But you are still very uneasy about going. Being away from your family and friends for a year seems like a really long time. What should you do?

Case Study Two

The person you have been dating for the past month is not a Christian. Your parents are not really wild about you dating at all, much less someone who doesn't go to church. Some of your friends think you should get out of the relationship; others have encouraged you to see it as a witnessing opportunity. (The person you're seeing hasn't shown a lot of interest yet, but hasn't been hostile to your faith or refused to consider it either.) What should you do?

Case Study Three

You're becoming a pretty good basketball player. The high school coach is already talking about making you the first ninth grader ever to play varsity. There has even been talk about college scholarships and other promises of success. Up to now, you had always thought you would go to a small Christian college. But it doesn't have much of basketball program. And basketball seriously cuts into your studying time for about half the year—keeping your grades up is a lot of work. You've been praying lately about whether God even wants you to keep playing basketball. Now the coach wants you to sign up for summer basketball camp—he wants a commitment this week! What should you do?